The Wea Engine

Contents

Features

Why are some places on Earth much hotter than others? The simple experiment on page 7 will help you understand one of the reasons for temperature differences.

Turn to page 17 and read **Diary Notes of Captain Smith** to find out what it's like to be "stuck in the doldrums."

You may have heard the saying "It's raining cats and dogs," but have you ever heard of it raining frogs? See page 19 for more.

Some scientists believe human activities cause global warming. Others believe warming is a normal climate change. Read **Living in a Hothouse** on page 26 and decide for yourself.

What damage can droughts cause?
Visit www.rigbyinfoquest.com
for more about CLIMATE.

Weather and Climate

Weather can change from day to day. Sunshine, rain, clouds, and winds come and go. However, the weather experienced in a certain geographical area is usually similar from year to year. These common patterns of weather are known as the area's climate.

Climate is affected by things that don't change, such as an area's position on Earth, its **altitude,** its landscape, and how close it is to mountains or oceans. Climate zones are regions that have similar kinds of weather. Scientists determine an area's climate by averaging its weather records over a period of at least 30 years.

There are four seasons—winter, spring, summer, and autumn—but not all climate zones have all four seasons.

In some tropical areas such as Vietnam, there are only two seasons, a wet season and a drier season. The wet season is in the summer months, and the dry season is in the winter months.

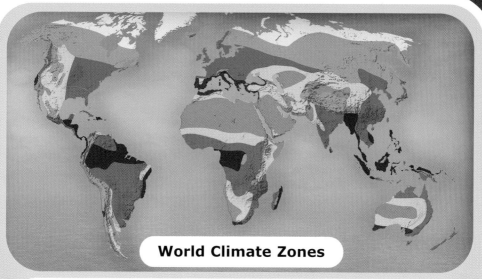

World Climate Zones

Key:

- Polar
- Northern temperate
- Temperate
- Mountain
- Mediterranean
- Arid
- Semiarid
- Tropical
- Subtropical

Polar zones are cold all year long.

Northern temperate zones have long, cold winters and mild, wet summers.

Temperate zones have four seasons, including mild, wet winters and warm, dry summers.

Mountain zones are cold, wet, and windy.

Mediterranean zones have hot, dry summers and cool, wet winters.

Arid zones receive very little rain. The days are hot, and the nights are very cold.

Semiarid zones are similar to arid zones with less extreme temperatures. These areas are warm and dry.

Tropical zones have high temperatures and high rainfall for most of the year. There is a short, dry season.

In subtropical zones, the summers are hot and wet, and the winters are cool and dry.

Driving the Weather

The energy that drives Earth's weather comes from the sun. The sun heats land and oceans, causing differences in temperature. This makes air move and winds blow. The heat of the sun also causes water to **evaporate** into the air, where it forms clouds and rain.

Different climate zones receive different amounts of the sun's energy, depending on their position on Earth and the time of year. In the tropics, the sun's energy is spread over a small area, and therefore the tropics are hot. At the poles, the heat energy from the sun is spread over large areas of land. The snow and ice at the poles reflect most of this energy, leaving very little heat.

TRY THIS!

In a darkened room, shine a flashlight directly at a wall. Notice how bright the light is and how much wall area is lit. This is like the sun shining on the tropics.

Now shine the flashlight at an angle. A bigger area is lit but not brightly. The light is spread out, as it is in temperate zones. The light that reaches polar zones is faint and even more spread out.

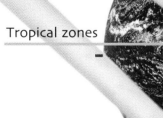

Tropical zones

Equator

Polar zones

Because of their position on Earth, tropical zones receive a higher concentration of heat energy from the sun than Earth's polar zones receive.

A Sea of Air

We live at the very bottom of a sea of air called the atmosphere. Earth's atmosphere contains oxygen for animals to breathe, it circulates water for plants and animals, and it keeps Earth warm enough for all life to exist. Although the atmosphere is over 400 miles thick, it is very small compared to the size of Earth.

Scientists have discovered that the temperature of the air varies according to its level in the atmosphere. They name the five different layers of atmosphere according to their temperatures.

In areas of high altitude, there is a lower concentration of oxygen in the air than there is in areas of lower altitude. Research has shown that athletes training and living in high altitude areas can increase their speed and endurance by 3 to 5%. This is because low oxygen concentrations allow the human body to use oxygen more efficiently.

The Layers of Earth's Atmosphere

Exosphere

The exosphere is more than 300 miles from Earth's surface.

Thermosphere

Thermosphere gases are very thin and absorb **ultraviolet radiation** from the sun. This area can have very high temperatures—up to 3,632 degrees Fahrenheit.

Mesosphere

The mesosphere is a layer of very cold, thin air.

Stratosphere

The air in the stratosphere is warm and dry. **Ozone** is found here.

Troposphere

Almost all of Earth's weather takes place in the troposphere because this is where the most **water vapor** is found.

9

Weather Watching

Mount Everest is the highest mountain in the world. Rising to 29,035 feet, it is part of the Himalayan mountain range on the border of Nepal and Tibet. On May 29, 1953, New Zealander Sir Edmund Hillary and Nepalese Sherpa Tenzing Norgay became the first people to reach the summit.

Since then, more than 1,250 people have successfully climbed Mount Everest. Sadly, however, many people have lost their lives on the mountain when rapid changes in the weather have trapped even some of the most experienced climbers.

Sir Edmund Hillary and Tenzing Norgay before their final ascent to Mount Everest's summit.

The Hillary Step

On May 10, 1996, a blinding whiteout storm hit near the summit of Mount Everest, trapping three groups of climbers. Although 24 climbers reached the summit that day, dozens became trapped on their descent by the sudden storm. With no warning, the storm brought gale-force winds and a very low **windchill factor**. It claimed the lives of eight climbers.

A "traffic jam" on the mountain may have been one of the causes of the great loss of life that day. Large numbers of climbers from different expeditions lined up to make their final ascent from the Hillary Step to the summit. This part of the climb is long and slow because it is technically difficult and exposed to the weather. Some climbers, therefore, had to stay longer at the top of the mountain than planned. During this time, the storm swept across the mountain and trapped many climbers.

Current Affairs

Tropical oceans are warmer than polar oceans because more energy from the sun reaches the tropics. Shallow water also heats up faster than deep water. This leads to differences in ocean temperatures on Earth.

Global wind patterns cause ocean currents that move in circles. The directions of the currents are influenced by three factors: Earth's wind systems drive them easterly or westerly, the continents drive them north or south, and the rotation of Earth drives their circular motions. A system of currents along the United States, such as the Gulf Stream flowing up the eastern coast, can influence weather as far away as Europe. This is because the Gulf Stream warms the westerly winds that blow toward Europe.

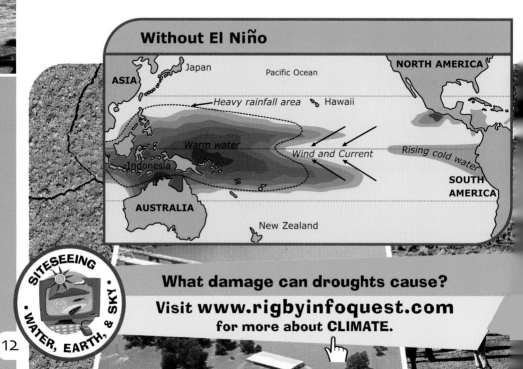

Without El Niño

Japan — Pacific Ocean — NORTH AMERICA

ASIA

Heavy rainfall area — Hawaii

Warm water — Wind and Current — Rising cold water

Indonesia

SOUTH AMERICA

AUSTRALIA

New Zealand

What damage can droughts cause?
Visit **www.rigbyinfoquest.com**
for more about CLIMATE.

SITESEEING · WATER, EARTH, & SKY

FOCUS

El Niño

El Niño is a weather condition that occurs every two to seven years and lasts about 18 months. It causes changes in the weather around the world. The waters in the eastern Pacific Ocean warm and cause clouds and heavy rain in the Americas. In the western Pacific Ocean, the climate becomes drier and can cause droughts in Asia and even bushfires in Australia. Since the early 1980s, El Niño has occurred more frequently.

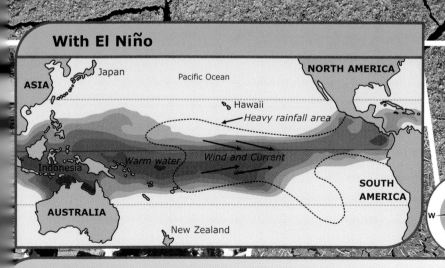

With El Niño

ASIA | Japan | Pacific Ocean | NORTH AMERICA
Hawaii
Heavy rainfall area
Indonesia | *Warm water* | *Wind and Current*
SOUTH AMERICA
AUSTRALIA | New Zealand

N
W E
S

During El Niño conditions, the east-to-west winds weaken and no longer draw cold water to the ocean's surface. Warm water and heavy rainfall move in an easterly direction.

Blowing in the Wind

Under Pressure

Scientists measure the force of air that presses on an area and call it air pressure. When air warms, it rises. This lowers the pressure at ground level, and causes a low, or cyclone. Above, the mass of air spreads out, cools, and sinks. This causes an area of high pressure at ground level, known as a high, or anticyclone.

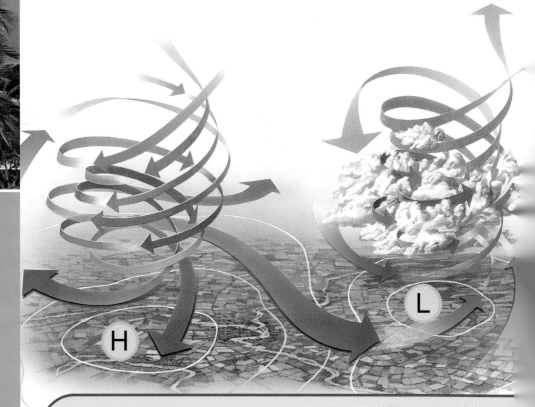

Sinking air prevents cloud formation, but rising air increases it. High pressure therefore, means clear, sunny weather, and low pressure usually means cloudy, wet weather.

Air moves from areas of high pressure to low pressure. We feel this movement of air as wind. The bigger the pressure difference, the stronger the wind blows. Wind does not go directly from high to low pressure, however. It gets **deflected** and spirals from the high into the low.

Winds spiral differently in different hemispheres. In the Northern Hemisphere, they go clockwise around a high and counterclockwise around a low. In the Southern Hemisphere, they go counterclockwise around a high and clockwise around a low.

In the Doldrums

There are regular patterns of winds at Earth's surface. Easterlies blowing toward the equator are known as the trade winds because sailing ships many years ago made use of them on trading missions. However, these ships had to be careful not to get stuck in the doldrums—regions slightly north of the equator where there is very little wind. Today, we use the word *doldrums* to describe a feeling of sadness or depression.

MY DIARY

Diary Notes of Captain Smith

Saturday, September 20

Finally, we are through the storm and the sea is calm once more. Our ship has been battered by strong winds and torrential rain. Now we must begin repairs.

Tuesday, September 23

Repairs are underway and progressing well, but now we have no wind. There's not even a breeze, and we're barely moving. I'm worried that if the wind doesn't pick up soon, our food and water supplies will begin to run low.

Monday, September 29

Our repairs are finished. We desperately need wind. My crew is becoming bored and speaks of doom and gloom. Being stuck in the doldrums is completely depressing.

Friday, October 3

Finally, a light breeze blows. We're on our way again!

Precipitation

The weather in an area of high pressure is generally fine because the air is sinking and warming. In a low, the weather can be cold and wet. When the air in a low rises, the water vapor in the air cools until it reaches the temperature known as the dew point, at which it **condenses.** This makes tiny droplets of water suspended in the air, which we call clouds. The water droplets might join together to form drops which are too heavy to hang in the air. These drops fall as rain.

A low blanket of gray clouds can bring a steady downpour of rain that lasts for an hour or more. Drizzle and light rain can last for much longer.

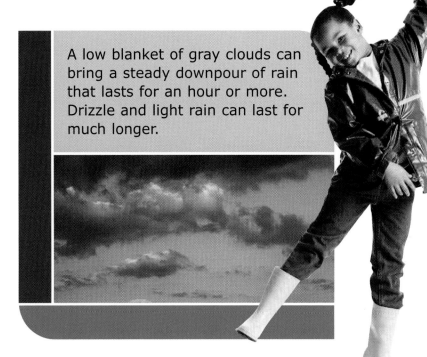

If the temperature of the air below a cloud is higher than the freezing point (32 degrees Fahrenheit), the water droplets fall as rain. If it is below the freezing point, ice crystals stay frozen and fall as snow or freezing rain. Hail only occurs in large clouds with powerful air currents. As the air currents swirl, layers of ice build up and hailstones grow.

Snow

Ice crystals

Hailstones

IN FOCUS

One night during 1883 in Cairo, Illinois, the decks of two steamships moored on the Mississippi River were covered with small green frogs about an inch in length. The frogs fell with a drenching rain during the night. It is thought that they were sucked up by a mini-tornado and then dumped to the ground as the tornado grew weaker.

The Lay of the Land

The shape of the land often affects the climate and weather of an area. Mountains force air to rise over them. The air cools and the water vapor condenses into clouds, rain, or even snow. This falls in the mountains, and the air continues on, warmer and drier. When this warm air blows down the other side of the mountains, it is sometimes called a fohn wind or a rain shadow.

The climate on the mountain itself varies according to height. The temperature drops with increasing altitude, so a warm climate at the foot of the mountain may be very different from a cold climate at its summit. Mountain passes can be very windy places. Instead of going over the mountains, air squeezes through the gaps between them.

Chilling Out

One of the strongest land breezes in the world occurs in Antarctica. At night, cold dense air from over the ice rushes out to the ocean at speeds of 100 miles per hour.

Have you ever wondered why snow and ice melt so slowly in the sun? It's because they are highly reflective. Most of the sun's energy bounces off the snow and ice rather than melting them.

Mountain and Valley Wind

During the day, sun shines on the slopes of the mountains, heating them and the air above them. This air rises, then cools, and falls into valleys. At night, the mountain air cools and flows down into valleys.

Sea Breeze

During the day, the sand on a beach is much hotter than the ocean. The air above the land heats and rises, spreading out. It sinks over the cool ocean and flows back to land to fill the space left by the rising air. Sea breezes mean that the beach can be a cool place on a hot day. At night, the land cools faster than the ocean, and cool air flows off the land onto the sea.

Masses of Air

Air particles move together in a big block of air known as an air mass, along with particles next to them that have the same temperature and moisture content. Air masses that form over tropical oceans are warm and wet; those that form over snow are cool and dry.

Air masses move around the globe all the time and often collide with each other. The area where hot and cold air masses meet is called a front. In a cold front, the cold air moves quickly and forces the warm air to rise above it. This creates thunderstorms, rain, and wind. In a warm front, the warm air moves slowly over the cold air, creating a wide band of clouds and rain.

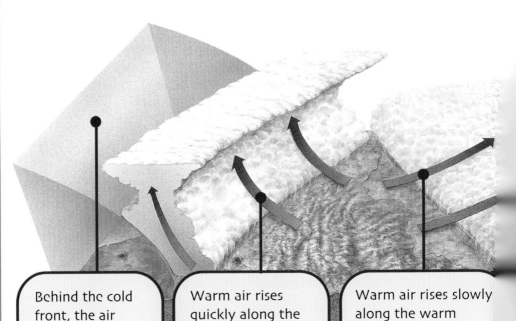

Behind the cold front, the air clears and the temperature falls.

Warm air rises quickly along the cold front, forming thunderstorms.

Warm air rises slowly along the warm front, producing widespread clouds.

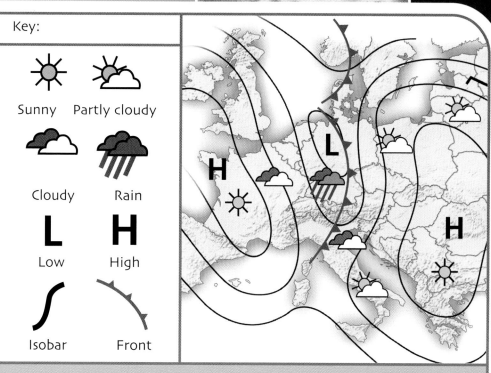

Key:

Sunny Partly cloudy

Cloudy Rain

L Low H High

Isobar Front

On this weather map, the areas of high pressure and low pressure are shown with black lines called isobars. You can see that there are two fronts where the hot and cold air masses meet.

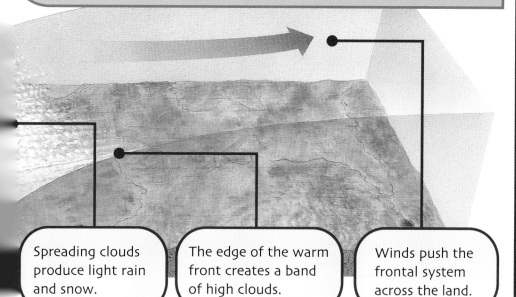

Spreading clouds produce light rain and snow.

The edge of the warm front creates a band of high clouds.

Winds push the frontal system across the land.

Forecasting

Weather stations located on land, in the air, and at sea collect data and readings of wind strength, temperature, **humidity**, and air pressure. This information is then fed into **computer modeling systems.** The computer plots the information onto a map, and a **meteorologist** must then interpret the data and write a weather forecast.

One simple weather report on television, on radio, or in the newspaper may have involved hundreds of meteorologists, complex computer systems, and huge amounts of data. A meteorologist's job is to turn complex scientific information into simple language that everyone can understand.

Polar-orbiting satellite

Radar station

Weather center

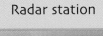
Research aircraft

Weather buoy

Geostationary satellite

Weather Balloons

In the early 1900s, balloons and kites such as the kite pictured on page 1 of this book were used to collect data from the atmosphere. Today, weather balloons carry an instrument called a radiosonde into the atmosphere to take pressure, temperature, and humidity measurements.

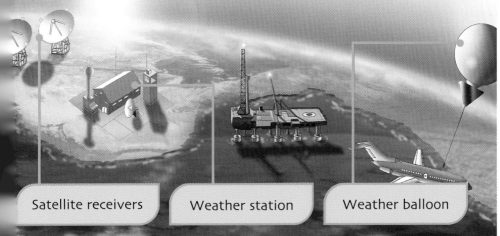

Satellite receivers

Weather station

Weather balloon

Living in a Hothouse

Earth's gaseous atmosphere allows the sun's energy to pass through but traps some of Earth's heat. If the atmosphere were not made up of gases, Earth would be far too cold for life to exist. If the levels of these gases increase, however, the temperature of Earth will continue to rise. This could cause changes in ocean levels and lead to wild weather all over the world.

Many scientists believe that we have caused global warming by burning fossil fuels such as coal, oil, and natural gas. They also think that cutting down forests caused more gases to be trapped in Earth's atmosphere. This has unnaturally raised the temperature of Earth's surface.

Some scientists are now saying that the increase in gases hasn't made any lasting difference to Earth's temperature or climate. They say that Earth's temperature has always gone up and down over centuries, and right now, the temperature is increasing slightly as it has in the past.

Wondrous Weather

Sometimes elements of the weather come together to put on a spectacular show. Rainbows happen when light rays are bent through water droplets, splitting the white light into seven colors. No two people see the same rainbow. According to their position, each person sees light bent at certain angles and through certain raindrops.

Beautiful streaks of colored light called the Aurora Borealis, or Northern Lights, and Aurora Australis, or Southern Lights, occur mainly at the poles. They are caused when electrically charged particles from the sun interact with molecules in the atmosphere.

A rainbow is not a physical object. It is an image of sunlight. A rainbow's center is directly opposite the sun.

Auroras appear as arcs, clouds, or streaks in the sky. Sometimes they move, brighten, or flicker suddenly.

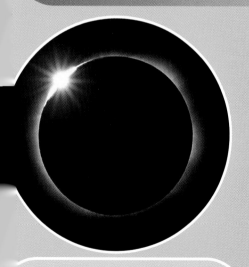

A solar eclipse can cause strong wind gusts in some areas and a total wind drop in other areas.

Many people are fooled by lenticular clouds. These smooth, wavy clouds can look like round flying objects.

Glossary

altitude – height above sea level

computer modeling system – a computer program that uses information to predict something happening in the future

condense – change from a gas to a liquid

deflect – to turn off a straight course and go in a different direction

evaporate – change from a liquid to a gas

geostationary – having an orbit that is at the same angle as the orbit of Earth so that the position above Earth remains the same

humidity – a measurement of how damp and moist the weather conditions are

meteorologist – a scientist who studies and predicts the weather

ozone – a gas made of three oxygen atoms per molecule. Ozone helps protect us from the sun's dangerous rays.

ultraviolet radiation – a form of energy that comes from the sun. Too much exposure to this kind of light can cause skin cancer.

water vapor – water in the form of a gas

windchill factor – a combination of the temperature and the wind speed that tells how cold the wind will feel to exposed human skin. A windchill factor of -18 or lower can quickly cause frostbite in a few minutes.

Index

Research Starters

1 The climate and the weather influence people every day, determining things such as the clothes they wear and the materials they use to build their homes. Choose three countries in different climate zones and find out the main kind of housing. Are there any special features used to design the houses that allow for certain weather conditions? Are some materials more suitable to the conditions than others?

2 Air pollution is largely caused by the burning of fossil fuels such as coal, oil, and natural gas. Find out how air pollution can affect the weather.

3 Find temperature and rainfall records for your area from the past few years and average them for each month. How do this year's average monthly temperatures and rainfall compare to those of previous years?

4 Find out what you would need to make a simple weather monitoring station. Then design and construct a station that you can use at school or at home.